# Garden *in* Transition

Printed in the United States of America:
Lightning Source (Ingram) Books Inc. (US)
1246 Heil Quaker Blvd.
La Vergne, TN 37086
USA

Printed in the United Kingdom:
Lightning Source (Ingram) Books UK Ltd.
Chapter House
Pitfield
Kiln Farm
Milton Keynes MK 11 3LW
UK

Printed in Australia:
Lightning Source (Ingram) Books AU Pty Ltd.
Unit A 1/A3
7 Janine Street
Scoresby, Victoria 3179
Australia

Cover, Design, Page Layout and Composition:
Lidija Markovic

Canadian Cataloguing in Publication Data:
Jones, Richard Merrick, 1947–
Jones, Connie, 1961–


Garden in Transition
ISBN:  978-0-9684857-9-8


1. Gardening – Canada  2. Flowers (Plants) –
Canada  3. Landscaping – Canada  4. Title
5. Jones, Richard Merrick  6. Jones, Connie

# Garden *in* Transition

RICHARD AND CONNIE JONES

This book is dedicated to our parents: Richard (Dick) and Lily Jones and Kwangyeon Kim and Dojin Choi, who loved the outdoors and were passionate about their gardens — they were truly inspirational.

Without transitions,
There would be no butterflies.

# Contents

Foreword   11

Introduction   12

Our Inspiration   27

The Transition   39

Urban Cottage   43

Final Thoughts   83

Acknowledgements   88

Endnotes   89

# FOREWORD

As proud owners of a suburban home, we appreciate all that the back garden has to offer. It is like an extension of the house, another outdoor room, in which to entertain guests and to unwind after the hustle and bustle of big-city life. We are fortunate that our backyard is totally private, which provides us an outdoor living space that is secluded and tranquil: truly a sanctuary.

In the more than 17 years we have owned the property, landscaping (decorating) of our outdoor room has become a major point of pride and interest. We feel the need to give as much attention to our outdoor living spaces as we do our indoor ones. As a result, over the years we have continuously added new elements to the garden and reshaped it. For a very long time lawn was a predominant feature, but a chance visit to a French garden opened our eyes to new possibilities.

Where grass once ruled, flagstone paths and patios are now accentuated. The stonework is not only visually appealing, but also requires much less maintenance than lawn and is more ecologically friendly.

What we have tried to do in this book is demonstrate the evolution (the transition) of our garden and the sources of our inspiration to make major change. We hope it will encourage you to think afresh about your own garden plot and explore ways to create an outdoor living space in which you can find solace and great joy.

Richard and Connie Jones

# Introduction

CHANGE IS A CONSTANT IN THE GARDEN; a garden is ever-evolving, never remaining the same from season to season or from year to year. You may have inherited a property you found attractive, or you may have devoted yourself, over many years, to creating an artistic landscaping masterpiece. But inevitably, plants thrive for a period of time, and then they perish or are transformed due to the vagaries of weather, pests and serendipitous gardening (Mother Nature's knack of rearranging the garden by having things grow wherever she wants them to). Plants move on, never staying the same for long.

Not only does the fickleness of nature alter the garden, but also, after a period of time, your interests and needs may change. After having invested so much time and effort in creating your ideal garden, and having developing an emotional attachment to it, it is often difficult to consider making radical changes; you can become paralyzed into inaction, unable to rethink and transform your outdoor spaces.

Connie and I are constantly reshaping our garden. When we first acquired the property in Richmond Hill (a small city just north of Toronto, Canada), the predominant feature was grass. The previous owner had transformed the backyard from a vegetable garden to lawn and had planted a few trees at the margins, so when we moved in, the garden was essentially a blank slate. In our first book, *Gift from the Garden* (2013), Connie and I describe how, over a period of a dozen years or so, we planted additional trees and new gardens along the periphery of the backyard, created an oriental garden with a concrete pagoda as a central feature, laid stepping-stone paths from the entrance into the backyard along the side of the house to the back patio and beyond, located numerous gardens and sitting areas throughout the yard, created a fishpond (complete with water plants and bridges) and designed and constructed a raised gazebo (which we call Tree Tops) from which to view the gardens below. The following photographs illustrate how the garden evolved over a 12-year time span.

TOP: The broad sweep of grass that was our original backyard.

RIGHT: Stepping-stones, bordered on the left by grape and chocolate vines and on the right by Japanese maple, hydrangea and Korean lilac trees, invite visitors to enter the backyard sanctuary.

ABOVE: Quiet sitting areas and vibrantly coloured gardens line the path, as it passes below the umbrella of a Japanese willow.

OPPOSITE: Waterlilies, corkscrew rushes and purple pickerel weed adorn the pond, as goldfish luxuriate in the shade below.

ABOVE: A cool-green, shady patio nestles into a private corner of the yard.

OPPOSITE: A rose and lavender garden is centrally located in the back lawn; a black locust towers over a waterfall and pond hidden from view.

ABOVE: A garden pagoda, brilliant-white in the mid-day light, keeps watch over a stream-like waterfall cascading through a mini-forest of evergreens.

OPPOSITE: The euonymus- and boxwood-lined stepping-stone path passes beneath a rose- and clematis-adorned arbor and meanders onward to Tree Tops.

I have to confess that although I do much of the "grunt work," Connie is the principal "author" of our garden, the one who is constantly "editing" it. I call her My Hummingbird, because throughout the growing season she flits incessantly about the garden, moving plants from areas that have become overgrown to others that need to be filled out or simply plead for a splash of colour.

We have always appreciated the soft green hues and textures afforded by lawn, and although over the years we had brought significant change to our back-garden sanctuary, grass remained an important component of it. But as much as we enjoyed our lawn (which was still sizeable), it was becoming increasingly difficult to maintain. We noticed that each year in spring the grass would emerge lush and green, but by the end of June it would become progressively thinner and begin to dry out despite a great deal of watering.

OPPOSITE: After a dozen years of transforming the property, lawn remains a predominant feature of the garden.

Also during May and June patches of damaged grass began to appear in the lawn, and sections of the turf were pulled up. Eventually, we discovered that our property was infested with Japanese Beetles. Female Japanese Beetles are attracted to moist, grassy areas to lay their eggs (so irrigating the lawn wasn't helping our cause). In due course, the eggs hatch to become grubs, which devour the roots, reducing the ability of the grass to absorb moisture, and eventually the grass dies. To make things worse, skunks and raccoons pull back the dying turf in search of the tasty grubs. Not just the grass was affected; once the grubs pupate and then emerge as adult beetles, they feast on many varieties of plants in our garden, most notably the flowers of certain roses and ivy leaves. We tried handpicking the adult beetles from the plants and spraying the affected areas of the lawn with beneficial nematodes that can control various soil-dwelling pests, but the problem persisted.

In addition, lawn care was becoming more labour-intensive and time-consuming. When it was one large expanse, I was able to cut and trim the edges of the grass in an hour or so. With the introduction of gardens interspersed throughout the yard, although I could still cut the grass in about an hour, another two hours was required to trim it at the gardens' edges. And I was not getting any younger!

Even though the property had its ongoing challenges, we adored our little piece of heaven and believed that through our labour of love, we were nearing completion of our landscaping *pièce de résistance*.

Little did we know that a sea change was in the wind!

# Our Inspiration

WE SIMPLY ADORE PARIS, and every time we travel to Europe we look for opportunities to visit our favourite city. In August 2014 we were fortunate to have such a chance, and having not done so before, we decided to take a day trip by train to the village of Giverny, located on the right bank of the River Seine approximately 75 kilometres northwest of Paris. Giverny's claim to fame is that from 1883 to 1926 it was the home of the famous French impressionist painter, Claude Monet, where many of his most well-known landscape paintings were created.

Monet truly transformed his property. The garden is in two parts: a flower garden called the *Clos Normand* – the walled garden – an expansive flower garden in front of the house, gently sloping to the road below, and beyond that, on the far side of the road, a magnificent Japanese-inspired water garden. Originally planted as an orchard, the one-hectare *Clos Normand* was converted to gardens, crisscrossed with a network of gravel trails that passed through banks of vibrantly coloured flowers such as hollyhocks, dahlias, nasturtiums, daisies, poppies and roses. Monet mixed commonplace flowers with more rare varieties and enjoyed exchanging plants with his friends. He did not subscribe to overly organized or contained gardens but rather combined flowers according to their colours and then left them to grow freely.

TOP RIGHT: Iron arches, upon which climbing roses grow, span the central alley, while nasturtiums invade the gravel pathways below.

RIGHT: Flower clumps of varying dimensions and hues give complexity, texture and vibrancy to the natural garden.

A riot of colour — dahlias, daisies, evening primroses, phlox, Himalayan orchids (balsam) and poppies grow freely.

My Hummingbird, enveloped in purple-themed gardens of dahlia, phlox, lavender, salvia, hyacinth, lupine, clematis — and wisteria overhead.

Ten years after his arrival at Giverny, Monet purchased the tract of land bordering his property on the far side of the road below his original gardens. The property was crossed by a small stream, which, after the first small pond was excavated, became its water source. Eventually, Monet enlarged the pond to its present-day size. Irregular shapes and curves characterize the lily pond, which was inspired by the Japanese gardens with which Monet was acquainted from the many prints he had collected.[i] Footpaths wend their way around the margins of the water garden.

The Japanese bridge is overhung by the long, drooping branches of a weeping willow, and everywhere the ubiquitous waterlilies (nymphaeas) bloom all summer long.

Unlike the *Clos Normand* where Monet dedicated himself to flowers, with the water garden, he was fascinated by the effects of reflections in water; thick vegetation surrounds the pond to create a secluded, tranquil enclosure separated from the surrounding countryside.

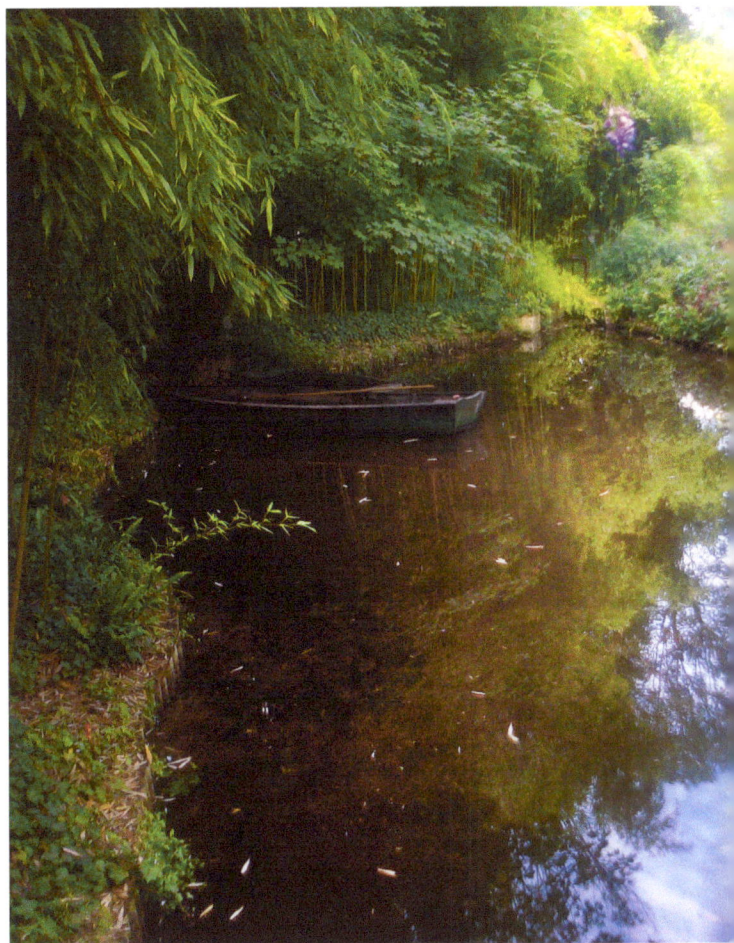

ABOVE: Here, the pond is stream-like; willows bow, shading the waterway's margins; waterlilies abound.

RIGHT: A serene corner of the pond, guarded on one side by an impenetrable bamboo grove.

That brief visit to Giverny changed our perspective on what a garden could be. We were impressed by the absence of lawn and the use of footpaths to allow people to fully experience and appreciate the gardens, while preventing them from disturbing the plants. Before we left France, Connie and I resolved to transform our garden immediately upon our return home.

OPPOSITE: Transparencies and reflections — an upside-down world transformed by water.

# The Transition

WORK BEGAN IMMEDIATELY. We returned from France at the end of August having already decided that the lawn was history, and that flagstone paths and patios would replace it. The first order of business was to remove the grass and enlarge the gardens. During the first week of September, Connie and I, shovels and trowels in hand, dug up every blade of grass in the backyard. We were shocked to discover that just below the layer of grass a shallow, horizontal system of tree roots permeated the soil. That was why the grass had been in distress during the summer months; the trees and larger plants had been stealing most of the available moisture!

In the week that followed, we ordered five tons of flagstone and two tons of gravel and limestone screening and raked the soil to prepare it for the stonework. Over a single long weekend in September, we completed our task. And what a team we made! While I wheelbarrowed loads of material from the front driveway, Connie spread the gravel and screenings and laid the flagstone to create the desired pattern of paths and patios throughout the garden. We appreciated the transformation so much that the following week we transitioned grass to stonework in the front yard as well.

# Urban Cottage

WE CALL THE BACKYARD (including a sunroom, which we consider an integral part of the garden) our cottage, because it is natural, somewhat rustic, and it is the place where we spend most of our leisure time once nature begins to stir after a long winter sleep, and the signs of winter dissipate with the warmth of the spring sun. The best part of our cottage is that there is no commute. Unlike those who travel for hours to escape the city for cottage country, with one step from the house to the sunroom, and then another from the sunroom to the backyard, we enter a secluded, serene environment where the cares of everyday life melt away.

In the following pages, we celebrate our concept of simple, rural bliss in an urban environment, and we attempt to convey to the reader our sentiments about the romantic idyll we have pursued through the evolution and transition of our garden.

The moment you pass through the side gate, duck under the vines rambling overhead and make your way into the cool interior of the entryway, you step into another world. The narrow flagstone path beckons you forward through a cavern of green: on the left, a trellis overgrown by grape and chocolate vines creates a shade garden of hosta, lily-of-the-valley and fern, and on the right, a wall of ivy, nettles and hosta. The rusty-red foliage of a Japanese maple provides a splash of colour in this otherwise viridescent tunnel.

Moving ever further toward the interior, you begin to emerge into the light. Now you are greeted by gaily coloured Japanese lantern, bleeding heart, coneflower, daisy, hydrangea, bee balm and evening primrose flowers. A Japanese willow stands at the top end of the entryway, which branches to left and right. You are intrigued by the lure of the unknown. What lies beyond?

Reaching the willow's shady umbrella, a stunning, panoramic view of the backyard emerges, tantalizing you with the thought of mysterious, secret garden "rooms" that must surely be waiting to be discovered.

The inviting patio and adjacent stream-like
pond create just the perfect atmosphere
for languid days in our urban cottage.

A pagoda stands as the focal point of this Oriental garden "room." The sound of splashing water, cascading out from under the cover of evergreens, is soothing, relaxing and inviting, producing an oasis of serenity in the midst of the city.

Thick colonies of waterlilies rise on their stalks, reaching for the sun. Opening during the morning and early afternoon, fragrant flowers of pink, yellow, red, cream and white adorn this peaceful water feature.

ABOVE: The vivid, iridescent combinations of the dragonfly's yellow, green, brown and black hues at pond's edge.

Follow the stone footpath lined with the vibrant purples, yellows, pinks and whites of coneflowers, black-eyed Susans, phlox, and Himalayan orchids/balsam. Or select another route — through the clematis-crowned trellis, boxwood hedges and a sea of brilliant colour — to Tree Tops. The flowers' sweet aroma permeates the air.

Wildly different and breathtakingly beautiful, each garden "room" displays, through the selection of plants and colours, its own unique mood or theme. Tulips, phlox and stonecrops kindle the thrill of springtime and herald the arrival of another glorious season out of doors.

Pause for a moment and delight in the myriad of colours and scents that spring flowers have to offer.

Sitting areas abound and are strategically located throughout the garden for observing and appreciating the natural splendor from a variety of perspectives and for quiet contemplation. Roses, geraniums, black-eyed Susans, monkshood, lavender, poppies and the oh-so-vibrant greenery provide the paint for this vivid canvas.

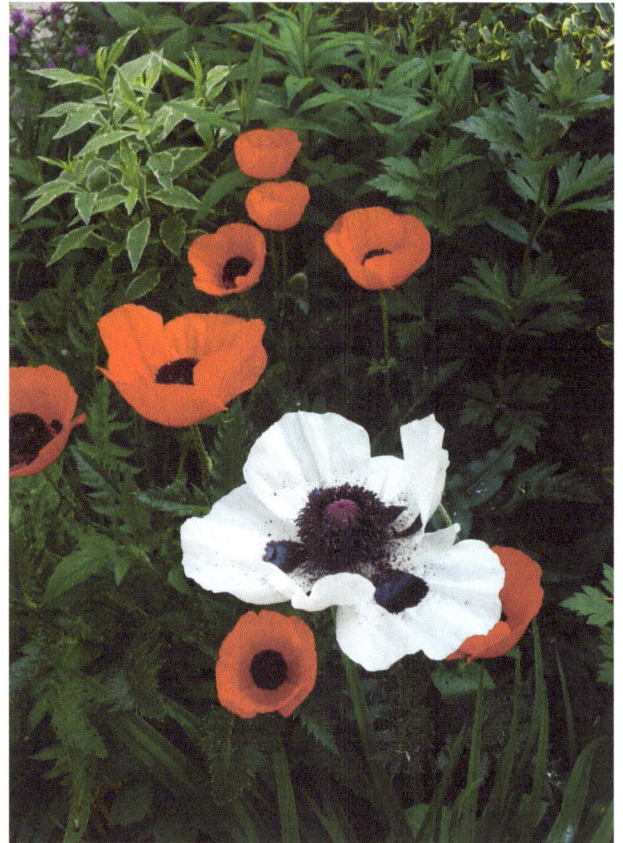

Poppies: showy, charismatic members of the garden family.

A cozy, secluded conversation "room" tucked into a corner of the backyard, shaded by the canopy of a cherry tree, enclosed on two sides by walls of ivy and accented by exuberant splashes of colour where the paths open into the central garden.

RIGHT: If tulips, phlox and stonecrops are the harbingers of spring, then our anemones are its confirmation. The sight of shady garden patches, brightened by their glistening white petals on a sunny day, leaves no doubt that spring has truly arrived.

OPPOSITE: Columbines, favourites of hummingbirds, are among our best-loved plants. They are truly unique: so delicate and orchid-like with their nodding, spurred flowers that come in an array of striking colours.

Stroll along the winding pathways, and wander from "room" to "room" to appreciate the French country-style garden with its combination of many-hued, eye-catching cottage-style gardens (some formal, some semi-wild), carefully trimmed hedges and stone landscaping.

Another tranquil thoughtful spot, set within a stunning milieu of phlox, morning glory and painter's palette.

Nettles, mosses, creeping Jenny and Stonecrop invade the narrow pathways, as they wind through gardens shaded by black locust and cherry trees. In early summer, the intense fragrance of black locust flowers (reminiscent of orange or vanilla blossoms) wafts throughout the property.

Early in the season, the Japanese willow is overspread with delicate pinky-white leaves; Miss Kim Korean lilacs  show off their incredibly fragrant purple blooms; and the arching stems of the weigela bush are covered in bell-shaped, crimson flowers.

In summer, pink roses, black-eyed Susans, purple phlox, blue hydrangeas, rusty-red and yellow daylilies, multi-coloured painter's palette and violet morning glories have their "day in the sun."

ABOVE: Follow the narrow footpath through flower clumps of various dimensions and colours that create a multi-textured, French-inspired country garden.

OPPOSITE: Another partially concealed conversation area, with a sheltered backdrop of French lilacs, overlooks a profusion of colour.

LEFT: An orientally inspired sitting area, accompanied by a functioning concrete lantern, is positioned just off to the side of the entry path. The remnants of a plum tree serve as a lattice for honeysuckle vines with their highly perfumed, trumpet-shaped flowers.

OPPOSITE: A red cedar trellis eventually replaces the remains of the aged plum.

# Final Thoughts

THERE IS SOMETHING ABOUT GARDENING that is unlike anything else one can experience. Quite apart from the well-known physical and mental health benefits derived from gardening, different garden styles can evoke all kinds of emotions and moods influenced by shape/layout, fragrance and colour. For example, formal, orderly gardens can have a calming, soothing effect; free-flowing, natural and semi-wild designs can create a sense of freedom and romance; quirky, creative gardens can be fun-loving, entertaining and thought-provoking; cozy, private spaces can be warm and welcoming, producing feelings of restfulness and serenity; the enchanting bouquet of fragrant blossoms can reduce anxiety and make us more contented; striking floral colours can be energizing, exciting and uplifting.[ii]

We have found that gardening helps us unwind after the stresses of everyday city life and enables us to establish a bond with nature – our greatest gift – which must be appreciated and nurtured. Alfred Austin (1835–1913) describes his feelings about gardening in the following way.

*"The glory of gardening: hands*
*in the dirt, head in the sun,*
*heart with nature. To nurture*
*a garden is to feed not just*
*the body, but the soul."*

We have attempted, through this book, to convey our passion for gardening and the deep appreciation and reverence we have for nature. We hope you have been encouraged to reflect anew on your own garden and explore ways to continually enhance it.

In the early years, we developed the area around the pond on an Oriental theme. But over time our backyard sanctuary has been transformed into a fusion of Oriental and French country-style designs. There have been times when we believed the work was done and all that remained was to savour our landscaping artwork. But unlike a sculptor or painter who can finally perceive their completed creations, a gardener's work is never-ending. A garden is never finished. A garden is always on the move — forever in a state of transition.

# ACKNOWLEDGEMENTS

The authors would like to express their appreciation to the Claude Monet Foundation for granting permission to include photographs taken of the impressionist painter's gardens in Giverny, France during the summer of 2014.

We also wish to acknowledge and thank Raf Ollivierre for granting us the rights to publish two of his photographs taken in our back garden. He is credited by name alongside each image.

Apart from Raf's contributions, all of the photography in this book is the work of Richard and Connie Jones.

Connie and I would like to especially thank Lidija Markovic for her many contributions to the preparation of this book, including cover, design, page layout and composition.

# ENDNOTES

[i] Giverny Non-for-profit Organisation. Giverny Monet's Garden;
retrieved from http://giverny.org/gardens/fcm/visitgb.htm, August 31, 2015.

[ii] This information was adapted from the work of Janna Schreier; retrieved from
https://jannaschreier.com/2015/01/11/impact-of-garden-style-on-emotions-and-mood/,
December 8, 2017.

www.ingramcontent.com/pod-product-compliance
Lightning Source LLC
Chambersburg PA
CBHW041933160426
42812CB00105B/2635